Impressionism

JUDY MARTIN

Wayland

ART AND ARTISTS

Ancient Art
Art in the Nineteenth Century
Impressionism
Modern Art
Renaissance Art
Western Art 1600–1800

Cover picture *In the Dining Room* by Berthe Morisot captures a housemaid pausing during her work. Morisot was able to transform ordinary events like this into beautiful paintings full of colour and light. (National Gallery of Art, Washington D.C.)

Title page *Impression, Sunrise* by Claude Monet, the painting that gave Impressionism its name. (Musée Marmottan, Paris.)

Series and book editor: Rosemary Ashley
Designer: Simon Borrough

First published in 1995 by
Wayland (Publishers) Limited
61 Western Road
Hove
East Sussex, BN3 1JD, England

© Copyright 1995
Wayland (Publishers) Limited

British Library Cataloguing in Publication Data
Martin, Judy
    Impressionism. – (Art & Artists Series)
    I. Title II. Series
    759.054

    ISBN 0-7502-0977-1

Typeset by Dorchester Typesetting Group Limited
Printed and bound by L.E.G.O. S.p.A., Vicenza, Italy

The publishers would like to point out that where there are variations in spelling or definition regarding the artists and works in this book, the example of *The Penguin Dictionary of Art and Artists*, reprinted in 1991, has been followed.

Picture acknowledgements
The photographs in this book were supplied by: AKG London cover (background), pages 7, 12, 17 (right), 20, 22, 25 (lower), 26, 30 (right), 32 (top), 34 (left), 36, 40, 43, 45 (both); Bridgeman Art Library cover (main picture), 4, 5, 8, 9, 10, 11, 13, 14, 15, 16, 17 (left), 18, 19, 21, 23, 24, 27, 28, 29 (left), 31, 32 (lower), 33, 34 (right), 35 (both), 38, 41; Visual Arts Library 6, 29 (right), 30 (left), 39, 42, 44; Wayland Picture Library/National Gallery 25 (top).

CONTENTS

1 INTRODUCTION

Autumn Effect at Argenteuil by Claude Monet perfectly captures the shimmering, golden light, showing Impressionist landscape painting at its finest. (Courtauld Institute Galleries, London.)

When first shown to the public in 1874, Impressionist paintings were treated as an outrage or a joke; the title 'Impressionist' was awarded to the artists as an insult. These same paintings are now enormously valuable items, worth huge amounts of money in any currency. They are reproduced everywhere as prints, postcards and greetings cards, which appeal to millions of people simply as beautiful pictures.

In its own time French Impressionism was a revolution in painting. Now, with hindsight, it is seen as the beginning of modern art. The Impressionist painters' lively vision of a world full of colour and light changed the way people saw things. The pictures' thick layers of paint and brilliant colours altered the way people expected paintings to look.

Art history is often presented as a series of 'movements', each labelled and defined as if part of a progressive scheme. Like most things in life, an art movement usually contains unplanned or inconsistent elements. Although

The Luncheon of the Boating Party by Pierre Auguste Renoir typically portrays a lively group of the artist's friends. His girlfriend Lise is in front on the left, and fellow painter Caillebotte is on the right. (Phillips Collection, Washington DC.)

the Impressionists were labelled as a group early on, as people and artists they had many differences between them.

What brought these artists together was an idea that their art should represent the people, places and events they encountered in real life. To us, more than a century later, this is not a surprising or revolutionary idea. But it was certainly not how other artists were thinking at the time. Impressionism was part of a wider movement of history, in which France was

developing into a modern European country, bringing changes that affected everything in people's surroundings, and altering their customs and lifestyles.

The story of Impressionism reflects these changes, but the Impressionists were not making social comments, they were painters. Their pictures convey their enthusiasm for their subjects, their love of colours and the skills of their craft, and remind us above all that paintings exist to be seen.

2 THE FRENCH ACADEMY

Lost Illusions by Charles Gleyre. This picture was a great success at the Salon of 1843. (Walters Art Gallery, Baltimore.)

In the mid-nineteenth century, Paris was the centre of the art world, attracting students and artists from all over France and from other countries. The major art institution was the Academy of Fine Arts, members of which ran the École des Beaux Arts (School of Fine Arts), in which the most ambitious young painters learned their trade. Students had to have achieved a certain standard of drawing ability before they would be accepted at the École. There were many smaller teaching studios in Paris where they could receive preliminary training.

The showcase for French artists was an annual exhibition called the Salon. Any artist could submit work to the Salon, but there was a jury of academicians connected to the École who chose what would be included in the exhibition. The Salon attracted a large number of viewers and influenced the choices of art buyers and patrons, so the jury were able to promote artists' careers or block their progress. Similarly, awards and scholarships to École students were controlled by established members of the Academy.

This had created a system that allowed an elite group of academicians to permanently establish their own standards and preferences. While all around them industrial and social changes were turning France into a modern

Bonjour Monsieur Courbet by Gustave Courbet (1819-77). The artist pioneered a realist style, including a self-portrait, in this informal picture. (Musée Fabre, Montepellier.)

country, they stuck rigidly to traditional ideas about art that were influenced by the Renaissance and the Classical art of ancient Greece and Rome.

The main emphasis of academic training lay in developing drawing skills. Students spent months drawing from plaster casts of sculptures before going on to life classes, where they would draw nudes in classical poses. They copied from art of the past – drawings, engravings and paintings on display in the Louvre museum. They learnt approved painting methods that produced smoothly finished pictures, often in sombre tones and colours.

Paintings of idealized scenes from history and classical mythology were continually successful at the annual Paris Salon. These were considered to be the proper subjects for an artist's attention. Portrait, still-life and landscape paintings were also shown, but were expected to follow traditional styles.

By the time the Impressionist artists began to enter this backward-looking world, its rigid attitudes were already being challenged. But the Academy and the Salon continued to dominate French art well into the second half of the nineteenth century, and some of the key events that brought about change occurred as a direct reaction to their influence.

3 THE BEGINNINGS

The Terrace at Ste Adresse by Monet. The bright colours were probably inspired by Japanese prints. (Metropolitan Museum of Art, New York.)

By the 1860s, there were many artists and writers who increasingly felt that art should relate to the real world and reflect modern life. This approach was being tried by different people in different ways, but for painters the route to a successful career still required acceptance at the Salon. So a conflict was growing between old and new ideas. The desire for change was one of the main factors linking the artists who would become the leading figures of Impressionism.

Portable painting equipment

The Impressionists could work outdoors more easily than previous artists because of changes in artists' materials and equipment. The most important of these was the invention, in the 1840s, of lightweight metal tubes for storing paint. Previously, artists could either mix colours in the studio as they were needed, or put them into pigs' bladders, which tended to leak or burst when carried around. Tube paints were clean and easy to transport. Artists' suppliers also advertised prepared canvases and portable easels, purpose-made for outdoor work.

Portrait of Bazille by Renoir. This portrait captures Bazille's attitude of careful concentration as he paints. The forward curve of his body and tilt of his head focus attention on his brush. The picture is also interesting as a record of Bazille, who was important to the development of Impressionism, but died too young to make a major contribution. (Musée d'Orsay, Paris.)

An important meeting occurred when four young painters separately enrolled in the same Paris teaching studio in 1862. Claude Monet (1840–1926) had already had some informal training and was returning to his art studies after doing army service. Pierre Auguste Renoir (1841–1919) had worked as a porcelain painter in a china factory. Frédéric Bazille (1841–70) was a medical student and taking art classes part-time. Alfred Sisley (1839–99) had given up a career in his family's business for painting.

The studio was run by the academic artist Charles Gleyre (1806–74), who provided his students with the required life classes and copying exercises. Renoir, Sisley and Bazille were determined to learn all they could, but Monet was rather restless and dissatisfied. As a teenager living in Le Havre on the northern French coast, he had been encouraged to paint outdoors by an older artist, Eugène Boudin (1824–98), who specialized in landscapes and beach scenes. Monet was already accustomed

to a freer, fresher approach to painting than was offered by Gleyre's teaching.

Monet persuaded his friends to go out painting in the countryside around Paris. Compared to the gloomy, enclosed atmosphere of the Paris studios, the outdoor settings were a world of colour and light. The artists began to develop their own techniques for recording the landscape around them as they saw it, abandoning the classical restraint of Salon

methods. As well as landscape pictures, they made attractive, informal studies of each other, of the people they met and the places where they stayed.

Their friendship continued after Gleyre's studio closed and they gradually got to know more experienced artists, who drew them into the networks of the Paris art world. It was a small world, and one introduction led to another. They found support among other

Left *View of Montmartre from the Cité des Fleurs* by Alfred Sisley. Montmartre is now absorbed into the built-up centre of Paris, but in the 1860s the area still had a rural feeling. (Musée des Beaux-Arts, Grenoble.)

Right *View of the Village* by Frédéric Bazille. Bazille's open-air portrait was shown at the Salon of 1869. (Musée Fabre, Montpellier.)

The Barbizon School
A number of artists who were pioneering the practice of painting landscape outdoors were an important influence on the Impressionists' approach. From the 1840s, the leaders of a group working in the village of Barbizon, in the Forest of Fontainebleau south of Paris, were achieving free, spontaneous landscape effects in their pictures. As students, Monet, Sisley, Renoir and Bazille worked at Fontainebleau, and were given advice and encouragement by the older artists who painted there, particularly Charles-François Daubigny (1817–1878) and Narcisse Diaz de la Peña (1807–76).

artists who were interested in the development of new approaches. But because the established art institutions were so influential, Monet and his fellow artists were all still aiming for acceptance at the Salon. There was nowhere else for them to obtain official and public approval for their work.

In 1863, the Salon jury rejected so many pictures that there was a general outcry among the artists who had submitted their work.

Emperor Napoleon III took an interest and arranged an alternative exhibition to display the rejected paintings. This was called the Salon des Refusés. It was an important event for artists whom the Salon jury wanted to dismiss for not conforming to their still restricted standards. Notable among the Refusés exhibitors was Édouard Manet (1832–83).

Manet wanted official success, but his paintings showed an independent approach in both subject and technique. Instead of the careful modelling and the dark, neutral colours often preferred by academic artists, his pictures were strong and dramatic. They contained figures that looked like real people, portrayed with bold, confident brushstrokes and in highly contrasted light and dark tones. Manet borrowed themes and subjects from the works he saw in the Louvre, but reinterpreted them in a modern context. His pictures showed how art could relate to the realities of contemporary life, not merely imitate traditions.

Left *Music at the Tuileries* by Édouard Manet. In 1860, the poet Charles Baudelaire published an essay challenging painters to portray the details of modern life. Manet's picture of a fashionable outdoor concert was a response to this. (Musée d'Orsay, Paris.)

Above *Déjeuner sur l'Herbe (Luncheon on the Grass)* by Manet caused a great scandal in 1863. To our eyes it seems a fairly unremarkable picture, in a natural progression from traditional styles of painting. (Musée d'Orsay, Paris.)

Manet's painting *Déjeuner sur l'Herbe (Luncheon on the Grass)* caused a scandal at the Salon des Refusés. It presented a nude woman and two men, both wearing modern-day jackets and trousers, picnicking on the grass among a grove of trees. Behind them was another woman bathing in a pool. The idea for the picture came from a painting by Giorgione, a well-known Renaissance artist, but Manet's updating of the image was considered shocking. Even the Emperor described the work as 'immodest'.

Manet's *Olympia*, which was accepted at the Salon in 1865, caused a similar sensation. Its subject, a nude woman elegantly posed on a couch, was hardly unusual in the history of art. Again, it was the modern style of the picture, conveyed by the appearance of the model and her setting, that was thought so scandalous.

Because of this kind of notoriety, and quite unwillingly, Manet found himself a leader among the avant-garde painters of the time. He became the centre of a group of artists,

Hillside at Vesinet, Yvelines by Camille Pissarro. This painting represents the artist's lifelong love of France, its countryside and agricultural activity. It is a beautiful study of the light in the open countryside, emphasized quite simply by the bright highlights on the cows' backs and the dark shadows of the trees on the ground. (Musée d'Orsay, Paris.)

writers and intellectuals that met regularly at the Café Guerbois, in the Batignolles area of Paris where he had his studio. Café society was an important feature of French cultural life. Meetings in a social setting allowed people to exchange ideas about art, literature, politics and philosophy informally.

Bazille knew Manet through family connections. He and Renoir, Monet and Sisley joined the café meetings. Three other artists, who with them would form the core of the Impressionist group, were also regular attenders.

Edgar Degas (1834–1917) had trained at the École des Beaux Arts, travelled in Italy and exhibited at the Salon. Despite this conventional career path, he was interested in the new attitudes to art that were emerging. Degas was not especially sociable. He could be aggressive and obstinate during the café discussions, but his opinions were respected.

Camille Pissarro (1830–1903) and Paul Cézanne (1839–1906) had met at the Académie Suisse, a life-drawing studio which Monet had

Racing Horses Before the Start by Edgar Degas. Degas's early style differed from that of the younger Impressionists in that he used drawing as a base for his composition, rather than working directly with colourful brushstrokes. Here you can see the outlines of horses and buildings. (Musée d'Orsay, Paris.)

also briefly attended. Like Monet, Pissarro had a special interest in outdoor landscape painting, which was also shared by Cézanne.

Pissarro was somewhat older than the other artists. He always made a point of encouraging younger colleagues and his socialist beliefs underlined a naturally generous character. Cézanne, like Sisley, had originally been set on a career in a family business, but also decided to follow his passion for art.

These were the painters about to start a revolution in the arts. But one important player was excluded. Respectable middle-class women in nineteenth-century society did not frequent cafés in the evenings. Berthe Morisot (1841–95) was already an accomplished and independent painter, who had been taught to work outdoors by the well-known artist Jean-Baptiste-Camille Corot (1796–1895). She made her contacts with the artistic network through more formal social occasions and while visiting the picture galleries at the Louvre, and quickly became part of the new movement.

4 IMPRESSIONISM EMERGES

Lordship Lane Station, Dulwich by Pissarro. This is one of the paintings he made while staying in London, avoiding the war that was taking place at home. It is an early example of the Impressionists' fascination with railways, which were cutting into the landscapes of England and France as the rail networks expanded. (Courtauld Institute Galleries, London.)

Monet, Renoir, Sisley and Bazille submitted pictures to the Salon every year from 1865. At first a few of their paintings were accepted and occasionally found a small measure of success, but their work was also frequently rejected. Monet and Renoir were often short of money, and had to be helped out by Bazille and Sisley, who had generous allowances from wealthy parents. But they all wanted to have their work taken seriously and to attract patrons and regular sales. The idea of holding a private group exhibition was discussed, but they could not afford to pay for it.

Everyone's lives were suddenly disrupted when, in 1870, France declared war on Prussia (now part of Germany). The Prussian army advanced rapidly and Paris was besieged. Monet and Pissarro crossed to England, and stayed there until the war was over. Renoir, Bazille, Manet and Degas joined different branches of military service.

The war was short, but it resulted in much political change. Napoleon III was exiled from France and a Republic was declared, governed by a newly elected National Assembly.

Above *Impression, Sunrise* by Monet gave Impressionism its name. Monet said later that he could never think of good titles, so someone else made up the title for this painting when it was exhibited in 1874. (Musée Marmottan, Paris.)

Above *The Barricade* by Manet. This watercolour sketch describes the violence he witnessed on the streets of Paris in 1871, during the short period of the civil war. (Magyar Szepmüveszeti Muzeum, Budapest.)

The hardships of the Paris siege gave way to civil war on the streets, when a popular revolution known as the Commune challenged the National Assembly. The revolt was quickly put down, and the leaders were shot or arrested. With a new order established, things began slowly to settle down.

Bazille was killed in the war. Sisley lost his financial support when the family business collapsed. On returning to France, Pissarro found that most of the paintings he had left behind had been destroyed.

However, the traditions of the Paris art world remained in place. The artists were more than ever dissatisfied with the controlling power of the Salon and began to lose interest in trying to exhibit their paintings there. The idea of an independent group exhibition was revived, and this time there was enough urgency and enthusiasm to overcome the practical difficulties. The exhibition went ahead.

The main exhibitors were Monet, Renoir, Sisley, Pissarro, Degas and Morisot. Cézanne contributed three paintings. Monet invited

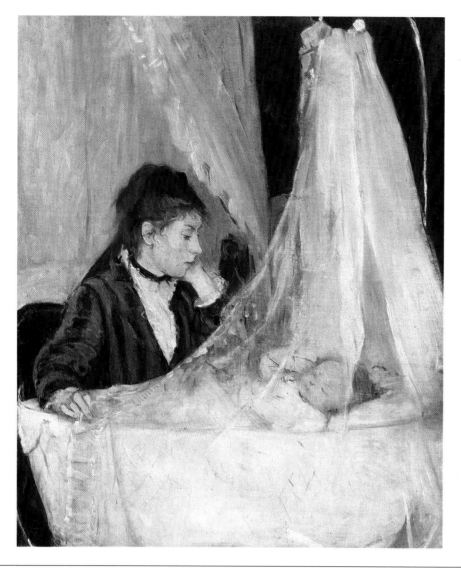

Left *The Cradle* by Berthe Morisot is a loving portrait of the artist's sister, Edma, and her new-born daughter. The painting was one of the few works that sold at the first Impressionist exhibition in 1874. The black and white contrast gives a strong pattern of shapes within which Morisot's delicate colours and brush marks re-create the different textures. (Musée d'Orsay, Paris.)

Right *The House of the Hanged Man* by Paul Cézanne. Despite the sombre title, this painting attracts the eye with its interlocking shapes and patches of bright light. But when it was first exhibited, Cézanne was criticized for the rough surface finish of his works. (Musée d'Orsay, Paris.)

Boudin to exhibit, and Degas insisted that some other, more established painters be included to attract public interest and give the exhibition respectability. Altogether, thirty artists took part.

Manet would have been an obvious leader for the group, but he refused to join the exhibition. One of his paintings had been greatly praised at the Salon the previous year, and he still hoped for formal recognition. He felt that direct association with the independent group might damage his career.

The exhibition opened on 15 April 1874 in a Paris studio belonging to the well-known photographer Félix Nadar. It was a risk, but the artists must have hoped for a serious response. Instead, they met with sarcasm and public ridicule. Critics seemed almost to enjoy attacking the work and proclaiming their disapproval. Newspaper reviews encouraged people to visit the exhibition as if it was a kind of sideshow, not an important artistic event.

A long article in the journal *Le Charivari* poked fun at the artists and their pictures. This unpleasant piece of journalism might have been rapidly forgotten but for one idea that lodged itself in the public mind. Seizing upon the word 'impression', from a painting by Monet called *Impression, Sunrise,* the

journalist made it the recurring theme of his article, which was entitled 'The Exhibition of the Impressionists'. The title stuck; the group was labelled.

The newspaper article described the pictures as rough and incompetent, talking about 'palette-scrapings' and 'mud-splashes'. Viewers were baffled by the busy brushwork and the bright colours. They could not see what they had been taught to expect in painting – the smoothly finished, orderly, storytelling pictures typical of Salon art. An impression that gave a broad overall sense of the subject and its atmosphere, without sharpening up all its detail, seemed meaningless.

A few visitors were stimulated by the exhibition and enjoyed the new work. Writers who already understood the artists' aims attempted to publish more sympathetic responses. In general, however, the hostile reviews seemed to far outweigh the encouraging ones. The exhibition had advertised the artists and given them a higher public profile, but it would be some time before this turned to their advantage. The spiteful tone of much of the criticism was upsetting, but none of the painters was put off. In fact, the second part of the 1870s was an especially productive time for the development of their work, in which the strongest qualities of Impressionism emerged.

5 PAINTING OUTDOORS

The Magpie, Winter by Monet. The title refers to the bird perching on the gate, but the snow was Monet's real subject. Notice the dashes of pink and yellow in the light, and the pale, cold blues in the shadows. (Musée d'Orsay, Paris.)

In traditional landscape painting, artists made sketches and studies outdoors, recording details of a view. They then took these back to the studio where they used the material to construct a finished painting. The sketches were free, like an impression, but the painting was usually highly organized and detailed. The painter drew a framework, creating the space and depth of the view, arranged a balance of light and shadow, and chose a set of colours that worked well together and created a harmonious effect. But the resulting pictures were often dark and lifeless, not at all like the natural countryside.

The colours of snow

Monet sometimes complained in letters to his friends and family that rain prevented him from working. But he loved to paint when it had snowed, although he described feeling frozen to the ground and having icicles in his beard. The Impressionists showed that snow was never pure white but, like water, picked up reflected colours from the land and sky, even lighting up the shadows. They applied warm and cool contrasts of pinks and mauves, yellows and blues, and tiny tints of pale and vibrant colours.

Red Roofs, Corner of a Village, Winter by Pissarro. This painting has an unusually crunchy texture. It was painted over a previous picture, so the paint had to be very thick to cover it. (Musée d'Orsay, Paris.)

The Impressionists were not interested in picking out features of the landscape and reorganizing them according to given rules. They wanted to paint the natural world as it appeared to them on the spot. In the vast space of a landscape, the things in view were not all seen equally clearly. Local colours – the colours that things actually are, like green grass, brown earth or red poppies – could appear to be tinged with other hues. The appearance and mood of the landscape could change in a second as a cloud passed the sun. Throughout the day, the intensity, colour and spread of the daylight altered continuously.

As they tried to capture the different effects they were seeing, the Impressionists used techniques typical of outdoor sketches. Masses of quick, short or flourished brushstrokes and dabs of colour laid side by side or one over another built up a complicated surface texture, from which a whole picture gradually emerged. Their methods were very direct and immediate, although sometimes they would adjust and tidy up the image, scrape off paint in patches and try again.

Landscape painting is especially associated with the Impressionists, but at first their

Above *Moret, beside the Loing* by Sisley. The calm mood is created by the low horizon and harmonious colours. (Musée d'Orsay, Paris.)

Right *Entry to the Village of Voisins*, *Yvelines* by Pissarro. The long shadows of the trees act as 'steps' into the picture. (Musée d'Orsay, Paris.)

outdoor scenes were often used as settings for people. A landscape or garden was not just a background, however, but as important to the overall picture as the human figures in it. Trees, fields, flowers or people were all viewed in the same way, as colourful shapes.

Some of Monet's most ambitious early works were outdoor figure paintings, but later he more often concentrated on the landscape. He seemed to select subjects almost at random, fascinated by the effects of light. In the course of his life he covered an astonishing range in his pictures, and experimented tirelessly.

Sisley, often working on his own, away from his friends, was the true landscape artist of Impressionism. He was always more interested in painting nature rather than towns and people, especially later in his life. Some of his pictures show signs of human activity, such as village buildings or empty boats moored on the river, but do not include the people who made use of them. Where figures do appear, they are often small-scale and loosely sketched, barely seen as separate from their surroundings. Sisley was not as inventive or wide-ranging as Monet, and his palette of colours was often more subdued. But his work

provides a glorious catalogue of rural France and its different moods according to the light and weather.

Pissarro loved the agricultural landscape of France and often painted dusty roads leading through sparsely-built villages, or open fields with people working on the land. But he was also attracted to the variety of things in the landscape and the way the character of places could change with the light. Pissarro and Cézanne frequently worked together, sometimes on similar subjects, such as a wooded hillside with buildings half-hidden by the trees. But there was always a different sense of what Cézanne was trying to convey in his pictures and he developed a markedly individual technique (see pages 39 and 40).

Many Impressionist painters concentrated on the gentle, green countryside around Paris, but the artists also went further afield. Monet painted the wild coastline of Brittany and the warmly-coloured landscape of southern France, and later travelled to Norway. Renoir worked in Italy and Algiers, Sisley in England. Each new place offered its own range of colourful impressions.

6 LIGHT ON THE RIVER

Monet Working on his Boat at Argenteuil by Manet. In 1874, Manet made this vivid painting of Monet with his wife, Camille, working in his 'floating studio'. Manet's colours boldly match the brightness of the river. (Bayerische Staatsgemaldesammlungen, Munich.)

The rapid expansion of the French railways, spreading out from Paris, made it easy for the artists to get out of the city into the nearby countryside. The River Seine, flowing through the heart of the region, was always a focal point of the landscape. Favourite Impressionist locations were dotted all along the course of the river and its tributaries. Monet, Pissarro and Sisley made their homes in some of these places.

The artists' fascination with light naturally focused on the river and its reflective qualities. The sparkle of light on water dances through the pictures, speckled with brilliant colours picked up from the sky, trees and houses on the riverbank, or bridges and boats. In some works the river appears quiet and motionless, a mirror of dazzling light changing colour with the progress of the day, but Sisley also captured the threatening mood of high flood waters.

Left *Summer's Day* by Morisot. The artist also used a boat so that she could go out on a river or lake to paint. She made a watercolour sketch of this subject too, so she may have worked on the full painting back home in her studio, following rough sketches made from a boat. (National Gallery, London.)

Floods at Port Marly by Sisley. Sisley used subdued colours to represent the stormy weather in this painting of the flooded River Seine. His blues and red-browns, which made greyish tints when mixed, give an unbroken effect to the overall colour scheme. (Musée d'Orsay, Paris.)

Monet was so enchanted by the river that he fitted up a rowing boat with a little canopied studio with the help of his friend, the painter Caillebotte. Working on the surface of the water, he could be fully absorbed in its atmosphere. The studio boat also made it more practical to explore new locations on the river, as he could travel along the water armed with canvases and paints, ready to moor the boat whenever a particular view caught his interest.

Colour contrasts

Rather than rely on light and dark tones to give their images solidity and depth, like the effects in a black-and-white photograph, the Impressionists preferred using colour contrasts. This gave their pictures more 'sparkle'. They made great use of the contrast of opposite, or complementary colours – red and green, yellow and mauve, orange and blue – often using these colours against one another to create the appearance of light. For instance, they used blues and violets to colour the shadows cast by warm sunlight, which was itself tinged with orange or yellow.

The Bridge at Argenteuil by Monet. In his work at Argenteuil during the 1870s, Monet learnt to portray the river's luminosity by using dashes of bright colour and contrasting tones. (Musée d'Orsay, Paris.)

Pictures of the river provide glimpses of a changing way of life. Riverside factories or the starkly modern railway bridge spanning the Seine at Argenteuil show how industrial progress was spreading into the countryside. Bathing and boating areas, promenades and restaurants were used by working city people, able to visit the countryside on their days off with a little money to spend on entertainment. The lively shapes and colours of the figures added variety to the Impressionists' compositions.

A brighter palette

Pigments, the colouring materials in paint, were originally all obtained from natural sources, such as soil, rocks, plants and precious stones. Industrial development in the nineteenth century provided new sources of chemically-produced pigments, which included mauve and a brighter range of yellows, blues and greens. The Impressionists made full use of these new colours, often mixing in white to obtain bright tints. Instead of the dark-stained surfaces used by academic artists, they worked on canvases primed with white, so that their colours were brilliant and clean.

7 PAINTING PEOPLE

Dance at the Moulin de la Galette by Renoir is lit by scattered patches of pale sunlight falling on faces, hands and clothes. (Musée d'Orsay, Paris.)

Impressionist pictures are populated with a lively cross-section of French society. The artists painted their families, friends and patrons, and people they saw in the streets, parks and countryside. The range of the paintings includes outdoor views crowded with large groups of figures, the busy interiors of theatres and cafés, intimate domestic scenes of people's daily lives, and formal individual portraits.

Despite the Impressionists' emphasis on realism and direct observation, large-scale group subjects could not be fully painted on the spot. Each picture was like a freeze-frame from a scene of continuous action, and it might take weeks to complete a large composition. The arrangement of figures against a complicated background had to be carefully planned. For details of poses and gestures, the artists often asked partners, friends and colleagues to act as studio models. So paintings that seem to record a broad cross-section of society sometimes contain the same people playing different roles in different scenes.

Girl with a Cat by Renoir. In individual portraits, the artist paid close attention to the glow of skin tones. Here, he has mostly achieved this with pale, warm colours, but there are subtle, cooler mauves in the shading on the face. Renoir's light, feathery brush strokes work well for the soft texture of the cat's fur. (National Gallery of Art, Washington D.C.)

Renoir's experience of painting landscapes enabled him to create beautiful lighting effects in his pictures of people outdoors – the dappled light on dancers in the open air at the Moulin de la Galette, a Parisian leisure spot, or the soft lighting filtered through trees over a full-length portrait of his girlfriend Lise. His appreciation of colour variations in light and shadow gave a glorious luminosity to his subjects' skin tones and particular brilliance or delicacy to the fabrics and textures of their clothing.

Renoir earned some money from commissions to paint portraits. In his more formal portraits, made in interior settings, the direct lighting gives a harder edge to the contrasts of colour and tone. But the expressive character of his subjects is always conveyed through his keen eye for detail and the light touch of his brush.

Degas focused exclusively on people, and throughout his life he stuck fiercely to conventional studio practice. He wanted the time and privacy to compose his paintings

Miss La La at the Circus Fernando by Degas. Degas cleverly organized this picture to show us the view from below, and used rich and unusual colours. Miss La La was an acrobat whose most startling act was to hang by her teeth. (National Gallery, London.)

The Dancing Lesson by Degas. This is one of a series of pictures of ballet dancers, showing them dressing, practising steps, rehearsing on stage and performing. Degas has made an interesting composition, creating a 'snapshot' of the ballet class. Because the figures go right off the sides of the picture, you know that there is more space and activity beyond what you can see here. (Musée d'Orsay, Paris.)

carefully and work on the technicalities. But he made hundreds of sketches and studies from on-the-spot observation, of singers and orchestras performing opera, ballet dancers rehearsing or jockeys assembling their mounts on the racecourse. His studio-based pictures, however formally composed, always retained his sharp impressions of real life. He developed masterly techniques for giving a sense of movement to his subjects, which were also adapted to his quiet, intimate studies of women washing themselves.

The way Degas constructed his pictures was not at all conventional. He liked to take an unusual view, as if glancing at his subjects from above, below or to the side. He allowed the activity to spill out of the picture frame, so that fragments of faces and bodies appeared cut off by the edges of the canvas. These 'slice of life' compositions were influenced by the new art of photography. Degas noticed the variations of focus in photographic images and the random composition of snapshot pictures. He linked these effects to his painting methods, and

Left *The Cup of Tea* by Mary Cassatt (Metropolitan Museum of Art, New York).

Above *The Artist's Mother and Sister* by Berthe Morisot (National Gallery of Art, New York.)

sometimes worked from his own photographs and also from pictures that he found.

A special sympathy for private, domestic moments is typical of the work of Berthe Morisot and the American artist Mary Cassatt (1844–1926). Their models were often members of their families – Morisot's mother, sister, husband and daughters or Cassatt's parents, her brother and sisters and their children. The people are involved in everyday occupations such as reading, sewing, trying on a dress or looking after a baby. Morisot and Cassatt's special contribution to the Impressionist record of modern life was a true sense of what women's lives were like. Unlike many society women encouraged to dabble with paints as a hobby, Morisot and Cassatt painted seriously and were highly regarded by their colleagues.

Morisot's style was confident and adventurous. She had learnt from early experience of outdoor painting, and even when confined to the garden or the house, she captured the tones and colours of her surroundings with a brilliant freshness. Her brushstrokes flicker across every square centimetre of the canvas, sometimes making the paint textures remarkably lively and abstract, but the detail of real life emerges.

Cassatt's introduction to the Impressionist group was through Degas, who admired work she exhibited at the Salon. They became close associates and shared similarities of subject, composition and technique. A strong interest in drawing and printmaking gave their pictures a wide technical range. Cassatt's paintings and colour prints have many inventive qualities of line, texture and pattern.

8 IMPRESSIONISM IN THE CITY

Le Pont de l'Europe by Gustave Caillebotte, shows a road bridge spanning the railway sheds of Saint-Lazare station. The dramatically slanted perspective of the iron girders is emphasized by the angle of the dog's body moving into the picture from the very bottom of the canvas. (Petit Palais, Geneva.)

In the mid-nineteenth century, an ambitious architectural programme transformed Paris into an elegant, modern capital city. The crowded city centre was demolished and replaced by a carefully planned townscape of open boulevards, squares and parks. New housing and commercial zones were constructed, and public buildings, like the huge new railway stations, the Opéra theatre and the covered market-place of Les Halles, were built.

The new Paris reflected social changes taking place in France. Industrialization was altering the balance of the economy. A rising middle class of prosperous business people with social and political influence enjoyed the main benefits of the refurbished city centre. Factories and housing for workers were moved to the outskirts of a rapidly expanding urban area. People came from the country to the city looking for jobs, and the population of Paris doubled within twenty years.

The Impressionist artists all began their careers in Paris, and most lived in or within easy reach of the capital throughout their lives. Views of the city naturally featured in their paintings from time to time.

Monet and Pissarro enjoyed the broad sweep of the boulevards, a bright urban landscape populated with moving crowds, which they represented with tiny, dashing strokes. They chose high viewpoints, from hotel windows, for example, which spread out the streets before them. Renoir, always interested in people, preferred to take a closer, ground-level view of the Parisians' movements on the streets and in the parks.

Left *Gare Saint-Lazare* by Monet is one of a series of pictures of the new station. Monet loved the steamy atmosphere and the way it reflected the light filtering on to the glass-canopied tracks. (Musée d'Orsay, Paris.)

Below left Manet's *Gare Saint-Lazare* has the same background of steam clouds, but unlike Monet, he was not interested in atmospheric effects for their own sake. (National Gallery of Art, Washington DC.)

Buyers and patrons
In the many years before the Impressionists achieved secure reputations and regular sales, they depended on the support of several individual patrons. Among others, Monet was assisted by Ernest Hoschedé, a department store owner, Renoir by the publisher Georges Charpentier, and Sisley by the professional singer Jean-Baptiste Faure. Gustave Caillebotte built up a large collection of works by fellow Impressionists, partly to help finance his friends and also because he recognized the importance of their work. In his will he left the collection to the French nation, for public exhibition.

Each artist used aspects of the city to express individual interests. For Manet, the railway terminus of Gare St Lazare made an unusual background to a close-up study of a young woman and a girl, but the station buildings disappeared in clouds of steam behind a line of heavy iron railings. By contrast, Monet scaled down signs of life in his Gare St Lazare paintings, and made the steamy train sheds into monuments of dazzling colours. Each picture is alive with brilliant hues, brushed in with a network of small strokes.

The street architecture fascinated Gustave Caillebotte (1848–94), who met Renoir and Monet in 1874 and became a close friend. He used the crossroads, bridges and façades of Paris to structure his compositions. He seemed to have an equal interest in people and their settings. Caillebotte's style was more severe than that of the other Impressionists, constructed of straight lines and complex perspectives. His city (page 31) is hard-edged and grey, but shows the open townscape and clear light that are still typical of Paris today.

Boulevarde Montmartre by Pissarro has a high viewpoint that reduces the people on the streets to toy figures, dominated by the tall, elegant buildings of the new boulevards. (Hermitage, St Petersburg.)

There are also Impressionist views of London, another capital in the process of change. Self-exiled there in 1870 to escape the Franco-Prussian War, Monet and Pissarro kept up their habit of painting their surroundings. Monet created atmospheric views of the River Thames, its bridges and imposing skyline, a theme he returned to many years later. Pissarro was staying in the southern suburb of Norwood, which still had the character of a village. When Sisley later visited London, he preferred to see the surviving rural areas, as he did in Paris, looking for trees and green spaces that softened the urban geometry.

The Impressionists were alert to the qualities of light in different locations, but were not often interested in the pattern made by town buildings. Pissarro was the one who seemed to enter most into the life of towns, enjoying the setting and its activity, not only in his paintings of the Paris boulevards by night and day, but also the market-place and shopfronts at Dieppe or the streets and riverside quays of Rouen.

9 MONET'S SERIES PAINTINGS

Wherever he lived and worked, Monet always took his subject matter from his immediate surroundings. He would often produce a number of canvases on a chosen theme, or return to particular subjects or locations over a period of time. In the second half of his career, he developed this tendency into a definite system. He created large groups of pictures on particular themes, which became known as his series paintings.

The subjects of the series include haystacks in a field, a row of poplar trees on a riverbank near the artist's home at Giverny, the River Seine in early morning light, and Monet's own beautiful garden, in which he cultivated colourful flower borders and created large water-lily pools. On visits to Rouen, he rented rooms opposite the cathedral and studied its sculpted façade close-up, separated from its surroundings. There are thirty canvases in the Rouen Cathedral series, painted from only three viewpoints.

The true subject of the series paintings was light – the way it was reflected by solid objects or watery surfaces, creating clear patterns of

Left *Rouen Cathedral: the Portal* (far left) is an early morning view. Monet has used blues and purples lit by pale gold, cool light. *Rouen Cathedral at Sunset* has a golden glow all over, with the low shadow painted in a contrasting bright mauve. (Staatliche Kunstsammlungen, Weimer; and Pushkin Museum, Moscow.)

Above Monet's *Haystacks at the End of a Summer Morning* (left) and *Two Haystacks* (right) – have similar colour schemes to the Rouen pictures, showing the light at different times of day. *The Haystack* series was exhibited in Moscow in 1895, where it made a strong impact on a young artist called Wassily Kandinsky, who became a pioneer of completely abstract painting. (Musée d'Orsay, Paris; and J. H. Whittemore Collection, Naugatuck, Connecticut.)

Monet on technique
Monet provided a clear description of the Impressionist method:
> 'When you go out to paint, try to forget what object you have before you – a tree, a house, a field, or whatever. Merely think, here is a little square of blue, here an oblong of pink, here a streak of yellow, and paint it just as it looks to you, the exact colour and shape, until you have your own naive impression.'

light and shadow or filtering through a misty atmosphere. Different times of day and varying weather conditions appeared to Monet as new images, even when his subject and viewpoint remained exactly the same. He would work on several canvases at a time, moving from one to another as he saw the light change colour or the shadows shift their shapes.

Focusing on shape and form, Monet could explore ways of interpreting the light. The paintings progressed from descriptive views in his normally free, colourful style, to complex all-over surface textures crowded with brilliant hues. Monet allowed the images to evolve gradually to something way beyond the ordinary physical presence of the subject. The series paintings signalled the possibility of a completely new kind of art. Their influence was later acknowledged by twentieth-century painters who developed totally abstract colour paintings.

10 BEYOND IMPRESSIONISM

Water Lilies by Monet. This is one of many paintings Monet made of the water-lily pool in his garden at Giverny during his final years. In old age his eyesight began to fail and his paintings became more abstract, perhaps because he could see colour impressions more clearly than precise shapes. (Musée de l'Orangerie, Paris.)

Eight Impressionist exhibitions were held between 1874 and 1886. The second and third were still aimed at advertising the artists' work outside the judgement of the Salon, and were not much better received than the first. By the time of the fourth exhibition, in 1879, the artists began to find themselves accepted and were attracting greater support. After 1879, however, many different influences made it difficult for the Impressionists to maintain a group identity.

It took a long, slow build-up of exhibitions, sales and commissions before the major Impressionists could claim success. Patrons who supported them early on were vital to their progress. The most important of these was the art dealer Paul Durand-Ruel, who first met Monet and Pissarro when they submitted work to his London gallery in 1871. Back in

France, he was introduced to Sisley, Degas and Renoir. Whenever possible, Durand-Ruel bought pictures from the artists. His financial support was often crucial, and his faith in their work remarkable, considering that his investment took so long to pay off. As the Impressionists' main dealer, he was rewarded later when the pictures found their market.

Durand-Ruel organized the seventh Impressionist exhibition in 1882. Over the years, a number of artists had been included in the Impressionists' shows, introduced by one or other of the leading group members. Renoir invited Caillebotte to join, and Pissarro brought in Paul Gauguin (1848–1903). Degas's introduction of Cassatt was widely approved, but he later insisted on bringing in artists whom the others thought unsympathetic to their aims. Disagreements contributed to

Above *Woman in the Fields at Eragny* by Pissarro shows the influence of the younger artist Georges Seurat (see page 40.) (Musée d'Orsay, Paris.)

Right *The Umbrellas* by Renoir has a much tighter style than his earlier portraits and open-air pictures. (National Gallery, London.)

keeping some of the founder members away. Even Monet and Renoir dropped out. When Durand-Ruel persuaded the core group to reassemble in 1882, Degas did not exhibit because his newer artist friends were excluded.

At the final show in 1886, Monet, Renoir and Sisley were absent again. Pissarro was the only one to take part in all eight of the group exhibitions, and Morisot in all but one. But by the end of the 1880s, the original motive was long gone and the artists were finding success individually. An open exhibition known as the Salon des Indépendants had been set up in opposition to the official Salon. Impressionism was at last recognized as a highly important art movement. It was even becoming part of the establishment, as artists inspired by it went on to new styles of work that changed the rules yet again.

From the start the Impressionists were not a natural group in terms of social status or artistic aims. Degas, for example, never acknowledged the value of outdoor painting. The artists had come together mainly because they all opposed established practices, and in the early years they needed each other's support. Monet, Sisley, Pissarro and Morisot had a lot in common as painters. Renoir shared some of their enthusiasms, but never lost his love of older painting traditions. Cézanne did not really fit in with the group, and soon departed to pursue his work independently.

The artists' homes were in different places and most had families that claimed their attention. They led ordinary lives and occasionally travelled abroad to work. They often met when in Paris, visited each other sometimes and wrote letters, but were not always closely in contact.

After the Bath by Degas. The artist often used pastels rather than paints. This study shows the direct, energetic marks made by the pastels. (National Gallery, London.)

In later years, the artists' stylistic differences became more marked. Monet, dedicated to landscape, developed an almost abstract absorption with light and colour. Renoir, in complete contrast, abandoned Impressionist principles and looked for inspiration in the eighteenth-century paintings he had copied as a student, finally combining aspects of both styles. Sisley, Morisot and Degas continued to develop their own individual styles. Pissarro picked up new ideas and enthusiastically tried them out, but usually returned to something more like the basic principles of his earlier Impressionist work.

Even though the artists' impact on their contemporaries was first made by their work as a group, the diversity of the Impressionists is not really surprising. They did not set out to make history, only to make paintings that seemed in touch with their own lives. That simple idea brought these very different people together, creating a movement that far outlasted its own place and time.

11 POST-IMPRESSIONISM

Mont Saint-Victoire by Cézanne shows his 'geometry' of nature. The shape and direction of the brush marks and the slabs of colour construct the mountain and surrounding landscape. (Philadelphia Museum of Art.)

The term Post-Impressionism describes artistic developments in the late nineteenth century, focusing on a number of highly individual painters. 'Post' means 'after', but these artists did not come after the Impressionists chronologically, as they were broadly contemporary with Monet, Renoir and Pissarro. Cézanne is regarded as the most significant of the Post-Impressionists. Gauguin and Georges Seurat (1859–91), like Cézanne, contributed to Impressionist exhibitions and were closely associated with Pissarro. The other major figures were Vincent van Gogh (1853–90) and Henri de Toulouse-Lautrec (1864–1901), who were independent of the group, though influenced by the Impressionists.

Cézanne always had a greater interest in structures than Monet or Pissarro, and his early landscapes tended to reflect an organized pattern of shape and form. He sensed a natural geometry in things and set out to analyse how it appeared in nature, and how an artist could translate the geometrical shapes as a flat

Sunday Afternoon on the Island of La Grande Jatte by Georges Seurat. This was Seurat's largest and most ambitious Divisionist painting. He made separate studies of the figures and landscape, then put them all together in a formal, stylized composition. (Art Institute of Chicago.)

picture. He used regular brushstrokes that followed the direction of the planes and curves shaping his subject, and applied a harmonious order of colours to show space and depth.

In his final years, Cézanne constantly returned to a central motif – the monumental form of the Sainte Victoire mountain in Provence. As in Monet's series paintings, Cézanne's pictures developed highly abstract qualities, although his systematic paintings were very different from Monet's dissolving scenes. His methods had an immediate influence on newly developing styles in the early twentieth-century, particularly the movement called Cubism, which was concerned with ways of showing complex views of three-dimensional forms on a two-dimensional surface.

Seurat departed completely from Impressionism, and invented a painting system known as Divisionism or Pointillism, based on scientific theories about colour. An important element of Seurat's method was the principle of optical mixing, in which tiny dots of colour, seen side by side, appear to the viewer to blend.

He achieved a great range of colours and tones by varying the proportions of differently combined colours across different areas, keeping the dot pattern small and consistent.

In *Tahitian Pastorals*, Paul Gaugin used the same flat shapes and strong colours of much of his work in France, applying them to the subjects and symbolism of his Tahitian surroundings. (Hermitage, St Petersburg.)

The apparent mixtures seemed especially vibrant, because their ingredients were pure and unmixed. Colours such as green and orange or red and blue, which blend muddily on the palette, have a subtle influence on each other when dotted together. Local colours, such as the green of trees and grass, could be speckled with warm yellow and orange to provide light, with cold pink, blue and mauve to form shadows.

Seurat produced several beautiful, striking paintings, some very large and some quite small. But when he died at the age of thirty-one from a sudden illness, the experiment with a 'painting science' came to an end. The work of

his colleague Paul Signac (1863–1935) was less refined and his style changed without Seurat as a guide. Pissarro was excited by pointillism and painted in that way for a while. But he decided it was a dead end, and returned to his more vigorous Impressionist manner.

Paul Gauguin so admired the Impressionists that he abandoned a successful business career to take up painting, but he moved away from their realist influence. The major change occurred while he was working in Brittany in the 1880s, when he began to compose landscape and figure paintings in formal, decorative arrangements, using broad, flat shapes and strong, non-naturalistic colours.

Cornfield with Rooks by Vincent van Gogh. This was the last painting van Gogh made before he died. It is a lonely, violent picture, but his skill as an artist made the balance of colour, tone and texture work brilliantly. (Van Gogh Museum, Amsterdam.)

He also introduced religious symbols, giving the work a feeling of mysticism.

Gauguin spent the latter years of his life in Tahiti and the Marquesas Islands in the South Pacific. The subject matter of his paintings was entirely drawn from his surroundings. Some pictures are beautiful studies of local people and their setting, but most have deep layers of symbolic and emotional content, often indicated by the titles. Gauguin combined very fine observation of shape, form and light with a newly imaginative use of line and colour. His pictures were intimate and expressive, quite different from anything that had gone before.

Van Gogh's life story, which includes poverty, illness and eventual suicide, is almost as well known as any of his paintings. He has been cast as a stereotype of the lonely, troubled genius.

But in the hundreds of letters that he wrote to his brother Theo over the course of his career, a different picture emerges. Van Gogh was a thoughtful, intelligent artist, with clear intentions and an understanding of the background of contemporary art and literature.

The letters describe his delight in the subjects he chose for his paintings – usually the ordinary people, places and objects in his immediate surroundings. Van Gogh loved the materials of his craft and talked about the qualities of particular colours, explaining how he intended using them to put mood and emotion into the pictures. His patterns of vividly coloured, heavy, stabbing and swirling brushstrokes are instantly recognizable. He made many drawings in pencil, chalk and ink that are similarly alive with lines, dashes and crosses. Although some of Van

In the Salon at the Rue des Moulins by Henri de Toulouse-Lautrec. The picture shows prostitutes waiting for their clients. Sketches relating to this picture suggest that the artist worked it out very carefully. His viewpoint puts us at the same level as the seated women, so we are drawn into the scene, but their turned-away poses and bored expressions do not invite us in. (Musée Toulouse-Lautrec, Albi.)

Gogh's pictures are among the best-known in the world, the ambitious range of his work is still surprising.

Toulouse-Lautrec chose to inhabit a night-time world of theatres, clubs, circuses and brothels, producing colourful, artificially lit studies of performers, prostitutes and night-club patrons. The enclosed rooms, spotlit platforms and crowded dance floors gave him plenty of inspiration for unusual compositions, framing scenes in a way that drew the viewer into the bright world of each painting. There are clear echoes of Manet and Degas in the bold line drawing and dramatic contrasts of tone. His free, sketchy brushwork owed much to Impressionist techniques and the vibrant colouring was also influenced by Seurat's scientific approach. Like Gauguin and Van Gogh, Lautrec evolved a highly personal style.

Lautrec's inventive techniques are very striking. Like Degas, he preferred to sketch on location and tackle major works in the privacy of his studio. He experimented with combinations of different materials – using pencil, charcoal, pastel, gouache and oil. He painted on canvas, paper and cardboard. He also made many lithographic prints, some directly used as poster advertising for star performers and special cabaret acts.

Impressionism was like a door opening on to a new gallery of art. The breakthrough from traditional artistic rules to a real, direct experience of the surrounding world gave artists the opportunity to consider new forms of interpretation. Their ideas and experiments became the baselines of modern art. In turn, each generation of artists opened another door for the next.

12 IMPRESSIONISM ABROAD

Walberswick Pier, Girls Running by the English artist Philip Wilson Steer (1860-1942). The colours, brush marks and contrast of light and shadow all follow ideas first described by Monet. (Tate Gallery, London.)

By the 1890s, Impressionism was accepted as a natural vision of modern France, the paintings were enjoyed and their style copied, and the former rebels were turning into the elder statesmen of French art. The continuing importance of Paris as a cultural centre drew the attention of artists and collectors from all over the world to Impressionist art. With improved international transport and communications, pictures could quite easily be taken overseas for showing in exhibitions and for sale. In this way the influence of Impressionism began to spread outside France.

American interest in Impressionism provided important support even before the artists gained full acceptance in France. In 1886, Durand-Ruel organized a large Impressionist exhibition in New York, and two years later he opened an office there to deal directly with American patrons. Mary Cassatt acted as a kind of on-the-spot American agent in Paris, talking to friends and advising art collectors about which paintings to buy.

Other American artists, like Cassat, had come to Europe to study and sometimes to settle,

Above *Claude Monet Painting at the Edge of a Wood* by John Singer Sargent. This picture, painted in 1888, reminds us of the young Impressionists' habit of painting each other. It is a charming representation of the close friendship between the middle-aged Monet and the younger American artist. (Tate Gallery, London.)

Midsummer Dance by the Swedish artist Anders Zorn (1860-1920). Although the Scandinavian sunlight is cool and the dancers' clothing is quite sombre, this lovely painting echoes Renoir's earlier studies of dancers in the open air (see page 27) and has the same kind of joyful enthusiasm. (Private collection.)

creating personal links between the continents. John Singer Sargent (1856–1925) produced outdoor paintings and grand society portraits in a dynamic, colourful style owing much to Impressionism. He knew Monet and worked with him at his home at Giverny. A group of American artists gradually assembled in the village of Giverny, going out to work in the same leafy, light-washed countryside that appeared in Monet's series paintings.

From the 1890s into the early twentieth century, aspects of Impressionist style can be traced throughout Europe and as far afield as Japan and Australia. Interesting versions of Impressionism occurred particularly in Italy and the Scandinavian countries.

It is difficult to know whether this was the direct influence of the French Impressionists or merely the coincidence of similar modern developments in art occurring independently in a number of places. But it was French Impressionism that dominated the artistic changes of that period, and passed on its special freshness of vision around the world.

GLOSSARY

Abstract The description of a painting that explores shapes, colours and textures as things in their own right, not as ways of depicting the real world.

Academic The term applied to someone or something belonging to an academy, or following traditional principles taught in such a place.

Academy An educational institution promoting certain standards of training or practice.

Avant-garde French word meaning 'vanguard', applied to people whose ideas or actions are ahead of their time.

Boulevards Wide, straight city streets, often lined with trees.

Chronologically Events arranged in order of occurrence.

Classical Relating to Ancient Greece and Rome.

Commission A task undertaken on someone's specific request, or an instruction to do so. A patron may commission a particular kind of painting from an artist.

Complementary colours Pairs of colours that are quite unlike each other and create strong contrasts; for example, red and green.

Composition The arrangement of a painting: the way the artist organizes things in relation to each other to make a complete picture.

Contemporary Belonging to the same period, or living at the same time.

Dealer A person who buys pictures from an artist in order to sell them on to other buyers.

Diversity Qualities of being different, as between individual people who for some reason come together as a group.

École des Beaux Arts The major school of arts in Paris, run by the French Academy of Fine Arts.

Establishment A group or class of people having authority within a society.

Façade The front of a building.

Form The three-dimensional qualities of a figure or object.

Franco-Prussian War The war fought between France and Prussia in 1870–71.

Geometry In art, a shape, configuration or arrangement.

Gouache A type of paint made of pigment (dry colour) mixed with liquid gum.

Harmonious Fitting or blending together well.

Hue Another word for colour.

Idealized Represented in an ideal or perfect form rather than naturally.

Lithographic print A picture made by the process of lithography, a printing method for reproducing a drawing made on a flat stone or metal plate.

Local colour The actual colour of something, as it is seen in clear light.

Luminosity The quality of something that seems to give off or reflect light.

Modelling In painting, this term refers to the way an artist makes a subject painted on a flat surface appear three-dimensional, by using tones and colours to represent light and shadow on solid shapes.

Motif The subject of a painting, or a particular image that an artist uses in his or her work.

Movement An artistic period or style, that can be seen as representing change or progress.

Non-naturalistic Not resembling the real world; for example, as in a painting that shows its subject in unrealistic colours.

Oil-paint A thick-textured paint made from pigment mixed with oil, usually a vegetable oil.

Palette The range of colours that an artist uses when painting, and also the surface on which colours are laid out and mixed, such as a wooden board or a ceramic dish.

Pastel Colour in stick form, made from pigment mixed with gum and pressed or rolled into shape.

Patron A person who commissions work from an artist, buys pictures regularly, or provides financial support.

Perspective The science of showing objects in space on a two-dimensional (flat) surface.

Pigment The ingredient of paint that gives it colour. Pigments come from natural or artificially produced materials and are finely ground into coloured powders.

Pointillism A painting method using small dots of colour to build up a picture.

Printmaking Any method of producing a picture by preparing it on one surface and printing it off on to another.

Realism A style of painting and sculpture that seeks to represent real life, rather than an idealized or romantic view of it.

Renaissance A time of rediscovery in Europe, of ideas from Ancient Greece and Rome, that occurred in the fifteenth and sixteenth centuries.

Salon The large annual art exhibition in Paris officially sponsored by the École des Beaux Arts and the French government. It was called the Salon after its original venue in the Salon Carré of the Louvre.

Stereotype A description which gives the same characteristics to a whole group of people and denies them any individual qualities.

Structures Arrangements and inter-relationships of parts, such as in buildings.
Subject matter The scenes, figures or objects that an artist chooses to represent in paintings.
Symbolic Using images of elements, such as colour, to represent something else (such as an idea or feeling, which cannot be shown directly).

Texture The feel of the surface of objects and how this is represented in art.
Tones The degrees of lightness and darkness in a picture. A strictly tonal picture is similar to the effect of a black-and-white photograph, but in painting tones and colours are usually closely related.

FURTHER READING

Davidson, Rosemary, *What is Art?* (Oxford Books, 1992).
Powell, Jillian *Famous Artists* (Wayland, 1994).
Powell, Jillian *Painting and Sculpture* (Wayland, 1989)
Richardson, Wendy and Jack *The World of Art series* (Macmillan, 1989-91)
Welton, Jude *Impressionism* (Dorling Kindersley, 1993)
Wiggins, Colin *Post Impressionism* (Dorling Kindersley, 1993).

For older readers
Denvir, Bernard *The Chronicle of Impressionism* (Thames and Hudson, 1993).
Gombrich, E. G. *The Story of Art* (Phaidon, reprinted 1989).
Murray, Peter and Linda *Dictionary of Art and Artists* (Penguin, reprinted 1991).
Osborne, Forfar and Chilvers *The Oxford Dictionary of Art* (O.U.P. 1988).
Petersen, K. and Wilson, J. J. *Women Artists* (The Women's Press, reprinted 1985).
Wilson, Michael *The Impressionists* (Phaidon, 1983).

WHERE TO SEE IMPRESSIONIST PAINTINGS

The best collections of Impressionist art are to be found in France, especially at the Musée d'Orsay in Paris. This large collection of nineteenth-century painting and sculpture includes the work of all the major Impressionists and many of their most famous pictures. You can see Claude Monet's own collection of Impressionist paintings at the Musée Marmottan, also in Paris.

A number of regional museums throughout France hold small collections of Impressionist work, some dedicated to particular artists. These include: Musée des Beaux Arts, Dijon; Musée des Beaux Arts, Lyon; Musée Claude Monet, Giverny; Musée du Dr Faure, Aix les Bains; Musée Fabre, Montpellier; Musée de l'Atelier de Paul Cézanne, Aix en Provence; Musée Renoir, Cagnes-sur-Mer and Musée Toulouse-Lautrec, Albi.

In Britain, the best collections of Impressionist art can be seen at the National, Tate, and Courtauld Institute Galleries, all in London. There are also Impressionist works in the National Gallery of Scotland in Edinburgh and Burrell Collection in Glasgow; National Museum of Wales in Cardiff, Ashmolean Museum in Oxford and Fitzwilliam Museum in Cambridge.

In the United States, thanks to the foresight of American nineteenth-century art collectors, several galleries and museums hold very fine collections of French Impressionist art. These include the National Gallery of Art, Washington DC; Metropolitan Museum of Art and the Museum of Modern Art, both in New York; the Art Institute of Chicago, the Philadelphia Museum of Art, the Phillips Collection in Washington D C , and the Getty Museum in California.

Index